FROM SPORE TO SPORE

Ferns and How They Grow

JEROME WEXLER

DODD, MEAD & COMPANY • NEW YORK

Copyright © 1985 by Jerome Wexler
Distributed in Canada by
McClelland and Stewart Limited, Toronto
Printed in Hong Kong by South China Printing Company

1   2   3   4   5   6   7   8   9   10

Library of Congress Cataloging in Publication Data
Wexler, Jerome.
        From spore to spore.

        Summary: Traces the life cycle of ferns and gives
advice on raising them.
        1. Ferns—Juvenile literature.   2. Ferns—Repro-
duction—Juvenile literature. [1. Ferns.   2. Ferns—
Reproduction] I.   Title.
QK522.5.W49 1984   587′.31   84-3496
ISBN 0-396-08317-X

Many people think of dinosaur bones when they think of fossils. What do you think of?

Fossils are traces we have found of animals and plants that were once alive. They may be bones or teeth or shells, or imprints left in rocks, or animals and plants preserved in ice, or even insects preserved in amber. A petrified tree trunk is a fossil, and so is a footprint left by a dinosaur.

3

4

This fossil was found in a coal mine in St. Clair, Pennsylvania. It is more than 250 million years old, at least 100 million years older than the oldest dinosaur fossil. At that time, the land that is now Pennsylvania was part of a giant swamp. The weather was much warmer and wetter then, and the swamp teemed with plant and animal life.

When plants and animals died, their bodies sank into the oozy swamp. They decayed slowly and incompletely, because they were covered with a thick layer of debris, which protected them from the oxygen necessary for decomposition. Year after year, century after century, plants and animals died, and the ooze became hundreds of feet thick. It grew so heavy that water was squeezed out of the lower layers. After thousands of years more, in some places the dry ooze turned to rock—rock that now, here and there, yields traces of the plants and animals from which it was formed.

The fossil impressions in this rock were left by a fern plant. The word *fern* is an old English word meaning "lacy" or "feathery." It is used to name a group of plants, many of which have lacy, feathery leaves.

Ferns first appeared on earth between 300 and 400 million years ago, and for a long time they and their relatives were the main form of plant life. During those hundreds and millions of years, ferns spread to every part of the world that was not too cold or too dry for them. Living in different environments, they evolved into many different kinds, or species, of ferns.

Today there are over 6,000 species of ferns in the world. Only about 250 are native to the United States. There are no typical ferns. Some live in water, and others live at the edge of deserts. Some live on the forest floor, and others live on the tops of trees, their roots never touching soil. Most ferns are small, although some, in warm areas like New Zealand, Malaya, or Central America, grow between sixty and eighty feet tall.

Asplenium daucifolium *(top)*
Staghorn fern

Some ferns seek the shade of a deep forest, and others grow best in full sunlight. Some thrive in acid soil, and some in sweet, or alkaline soil. Some grow in rocky soil, and others in soil with clay or sand.

In general, ferns grow best where there is plenty of moisture and the temperature is mild. They have probably changed very little during the hundreds of millions of years they have been on earth.

Australian tree fern

pear tree flower blossom

8

Life on earth has changed, however, and ferns are no longer the most abundant plants on earth. Millions of years after ferns evolved, another plant form arose, plants with flowers. There are now more than 250,000 species of flowering plants, and they are the main form of plant life on earth.

Ferns and flowering plants both have roots, stems, and leaves. They differ mainly in the way they reproduce. Ferns reproduce by spores, and flowering plants reproduce by seeds.

Botanists, scientists who study plants, spend months and even years watching the way ferns grow and reproduce in nature. An easier way to start to learn about ferns is to raise one indoors in a home or classroom. Not all ferns grow well indoors, so what is needed is a "house-type" fern. They can be bought, already growing, at plant stores. But a more interesting way to raise a house-type fern is to get the spores, scatter them on soil, and watch what happens.

This package contains spores for a fern called Ocean Spray. Ocean Spray belongs to a group of ferns called *Adiantum*, most of which are native to tropical countries.

A botanist would never call a spore a seed, but many people do—even seed companies. Look at the mix-up on this package of spores. The words say, *"Look closely—Seed like dust."*

"Seed like dust" is the company's way of warning that the spores are very small. In fact, a speck of dust is many times larger than a spore. We "see" spores when we open the package because the individual, microscopic spores cling together and form dust-sized specks.

For a long time people thought that ferns grew from seeds that were invisible, and that if a person ever found one and carried it around, they also would become invisible.

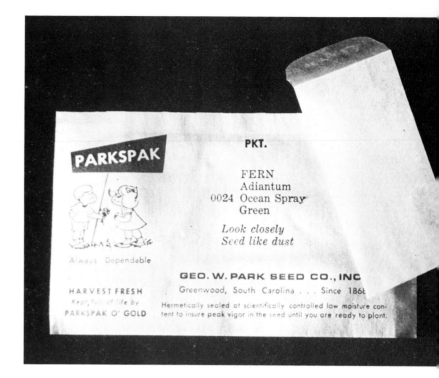

10

Both spores and seeds are the start of new plants, but they are not at all the same. Even the smallest seed is many times larger than a spore. A seed is a tiny, brand-new plant complete with its first baby leaves, surrounded by a watertight covering. Most seeds also contain a food supply to help the new plant start growing. When a seed is put into moist soil, the plant sends roots down for water and minerals. Then it sends its leaves up into the air for sunlight. Soon a flowering plant is growing above the ground.

A spore does not contain its own little plant, nor a food supply for growing. A spore is just a single cell, the smallest unit of life, with a sturdy covering around it. And when a spore is planted, it does not produce a flowering plant. It produces some other kind of plant. Spores from ferns give rise to fern plants.

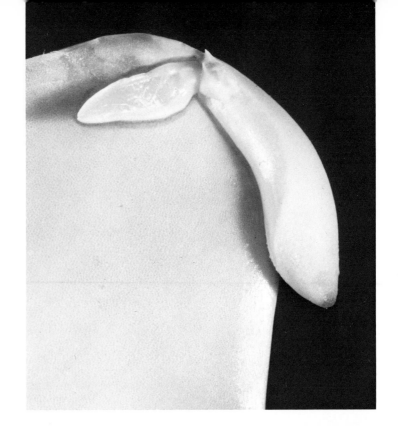

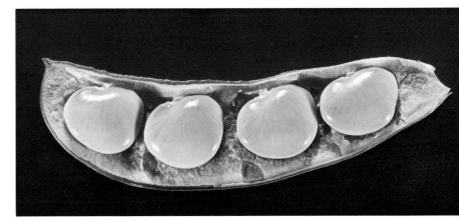

lima bean seeds in pod and cut open (top)

11

Let's plant some of the Ocean Spray spores from the package. We need just two things: a clean container with several half-inch holes in the bottom and sterilized potting soil. Backyard soil might contain insects, insect eggs, wild spores, or seeds.

We add enough water to the soil to make it moist but not soggy, then pack the soil lightly into the container. We smooth the surface and sprinkle the spores on it. If the top is partly covered with plastic wrap, it will help keep the soil and the surrounding air moist. We put the container in a warm spot with plenty of light—but not in direct sunlight, which could burn whatever grows from the spores.

If the soil dries out, the container can be put in a saucer of lukewarm water for a half-hour. Water will be absorbed through the holes. If we watered the soil from above, the spores would be carried down deep. They would start to grow, but without light they would soon die.

12

Here is what we see a month later. The ordinary straight pin shows how tiny these first plants are.

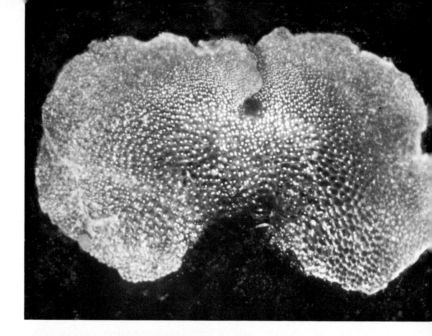

Each of the green leaf-like growths is called a prothallium. Two or more are called prothallia.

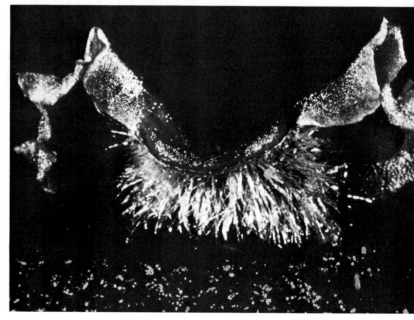

A prothallium is paper-thin and anchored to the soil by rootlike hairs, which take up water and minerals. Using sunlight, the prothallia change the water and minerals into food that gives them energy for further growth.

14

When the prothallia are about one-quarter inch across, they are full grown. Then something remarkable begins to happen. On the underside of each, near the center where the curved surfaces come together, a single female cell is formed. This cell is called an egg. In places along the edge of each prothallium, male cells are formed. They are called sperm, and they will travel toward the egg. The egg and the sperm are so small they cannot be seen without a microscope.

The distance from the sperm to the egg is only about one-eighth of an inch—a very small distance to us. But the sperm are microscopic, so their journey to the egg is a long one. How do they travel? A prothallium grows too close to the ground for the wind to pick the sperm up or for insects or other animals to transport them. Nothing is likely to get under the low-growing prothallium—except water.

When there is a drop of water between the prothallium and the soil, the sperm have their opportunity. The sperm "swim" to the egg. Many sperm cells may reach the egg cell, but only one will unite with it. The union of an egg cell and a sperm cell is called fertilization.

Because water is necessary for fertilization, it is especially important to keep the soil moist under our prothallia.

Scientists call the egg and sperm sex cells, or gametes. Because a fern's gametes are produced by a prothallium, a prothallium is sometimes called a gametophyte. "Phyte" comes from the Greek word *phyton*, which means "plant." So, gametophyte means "a plant bearing gametes." While the prothallium is growing, the fern is said to be in its gametophyte stage.

Each prothallium grew from a spore of the Ocean Spray fern. But a prothallium doesn't look like a fern. Ferns are more than one-quarter inch tall, and their leaves rise well above the soil surface. When will a plant that looks like a fern begin to grow?

Is this it? A new leaf is growing out of the center of this prothallium. You can see how tiny the prothallium is, and how tiny the new leaf is, by comparing them with the penny. This new leaf is the visible result of fertilization.

This first leaf is green. The color comes from a substance called chlorophyll. Only plants that have chlorophyll can use sunlight to change water and minerals from the soil into food that gives the plant energy to grow.

The first few leaves look different from one another. They are called "juvenile" leaves, and they help make food so the plant can keep growing. But it also gets nourishment from its parent—the prothallium.

Does it look like a fern yet?

As the new plant develops more leaves, it also puts down roots. After a while it no longer needs its parent. The prothallium begins to die—it dries up and turns a dark color. Here you can see the dying prothallium at the base of the leaves.

Now this is more like it. Our plant is beginning to look like something—a real fern.

The botanists who first studied ferns called their leaves "fronds." But there is no real difference between a leaf and a frond.

A frond is divided into two main parts: the stem and the blade. The stem is called the stipe. The whole leafy part is called the blade.

blade

stipe

The blade can be shaped in different ways. It can be solid like this one on the Bird's-nest fern—a simple blade.

Nephrolepis exaltata

Or, it can be divided into sections like this one—a compound blade. Each section in a compound blade is called a pinna.

If each pinna is further divided, those sections are called pinnules, and the blade is a twice-compound, like this *Asplenium daucifolium*.

The leaves on an Ocean Spray fern are twice-compound.

When a botanist is given an unknown plant and asked to identify it, he or she looks for clues that will place it in one of the major plant groups. Is it a flowering plant or a non-flowering plant? Is it one of the grasses? Is it a tree that loses its leaves in the fall or is it an evergreen?

One clue that helps identify ferns is the shape of the veins in their fronds. In the Ocean Spray fern they continually branch in a Y-shaped pattern.

25

Here is our fern six months later.

More time has gone by. Our Ocean Spray fern is a year old, and like most ferns, looks very graceful.

Another year has passed, and our plant is now two years old. For two years it has been growing indoors under almost ideal conditions. A humidifier has kept the room moist. The soil has been kept damp and the fronds have been sprayed lightly with water, to wash them and help keep the air around the plant humid. A fluorescent grow lamp has been on sixteen hours a day. Once a month the plant has been fed plant food made just for ferns.

When plants grow outdoors, they receive many "signals" from nature. As the seasons start to change, a wet area may become dry as a desert, or a dry area may become damp as a swamp. Temperatures may go up or down, days may get longer or shorter, sunlight may get stronger or weaker. Any one of these signals, or a combination of them, tells the plant that the environment is changing and that it too must change its growing habits.

Garden-grown mums, for example, produce flowers in the late fall, as the days get shorter. Plant nurseries use this knowledge to force their mums to flower in early spring, in time for Mother's Day. They imitate the short days of fall by covering their greenhouses with a black cloth every afternoon.

But in a home or a classroom, plants don't receive natural signals. When it gets cold outside, there is heat on inside. Though it may be night outside, inside the lights are bright.

Let's send our fern a signal by changing something in its indoor environment. Let's reduce the humidity in the room and also stop watering the plant for a month. What will happen?

At the end of the month, many of the fronds are dead. In fact, the plant itself looks more dead than alive.

Once we resume watering, new fronds begin to grow. But something strange has happened. Look closely. Some of the new fronds have spots around their edges.

People who see these spots for the first time often think the fern has a disease or has been attacked by an insect. Neither is true.

Each spot is a sort of little package wrapped in a thin membrane. A single spot is called a sorus; more than one are called sori.

Can you guess what the sori contain?

Those round shapes within the sorus are too big to be spores. But spores are forming inside of them. What you see are spore cases, called sporangia.

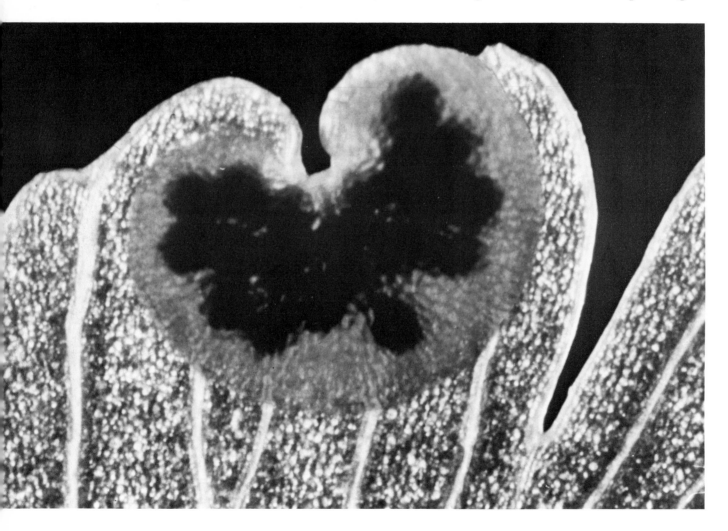

When the spores are mature, the membranes turn brown and lift off the surface of the frond. Then the sporangia explode, scattering microscopic spores in the air.

If we held one of these fronds in our hands, we would need a strong magnifying glass to see the sporangia burst open.

The dark spot by the upper right side of the penny is only *two* sporangia.

Spores can be harvested by laying the plant on its side with a large sheet of white paper under the fronds. (It is best to do this in a room where there is little air movement.) After a few days, a grayish dust collects on the paper—the spores.

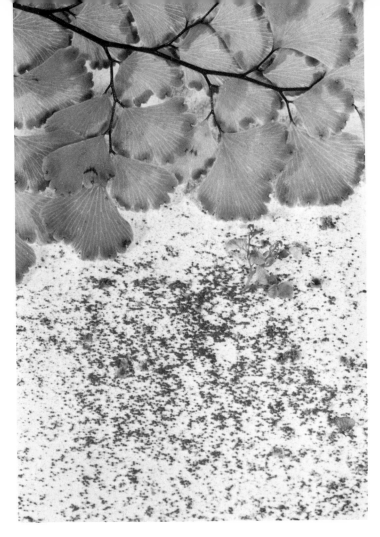

Here the fronds were violently shaken to release more spores. The collection on the paper consists of sori, sporangia, and spores. They can be stored in an envelope —or planted immediately.

On some ferns, like our Ocean Spray, sori appear on most of the fronds. On other ferns, like this one, sori are produced only by special fronds. Either way, fronds that bear sori are called fertile fronds.

All of the sori produced by one species of fern look alike. But sori of different species vary in color, size, pattern, and location—so much so that sori are a way to tell one kind of fern from another. These pages show sori of different species.

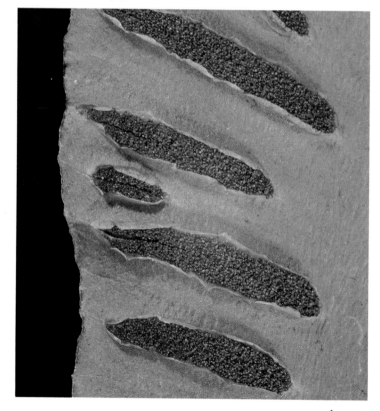

Scolopendrium fern

close up

36

A botanist says that a fern with sori is a "sporophyte"—a plant bearing spores. In fact, it makes no difference whether there are sori on the fronds or not. If the fern *could* produce spores on its fronds, then it is in its sporophyte stage.

The gametophyte stage usually lasts no longer than several months, but the sporophyte stage can last for many years. Most fronds do not die after producing sori. They die from old age and are replaced by new fronds. On ferns that live in cold areas, fronds may be "winter killed," but the plants themselves survive and produce new fronds in the spring.

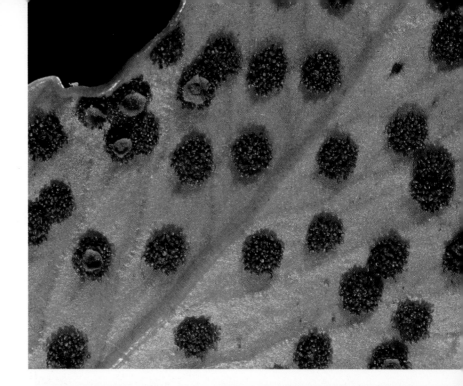

Holly fern (Cyrtomium falcatum) *(top)*
Table fern (Pteris evergemensis)

Our Ocean Spray fern, more than two feet across

The spore-bearing stage of our Ocean Spray fern—the phase that actually looks like a fern—grew out of the union of a sperm and the egg on the underside of a prothallium. And the prothallium grew from one of the spores we scattered on soil. So, the spores we planted eventually gave rise to a plant that makes more spores—from spore to spore. That is one way ferns have survived on earth for hundreds of millions of years.

If a single fern produces a billion spores in its lifetime, why isn't the world overrun with ferns? First of all, only some of those spores land in places where they can grow. And even then, a spore's growth is not a simple matter. The spore itself contains no food for the prothallium that will grow from it. The prothallium must get everything it needs from the world around it. Soil, sun, and water conditions must be exactly right, or it will not survive. And the prothallium is delicate—most of it is only one cell thick. Add to this the possible problems from weather, insects, disease, and competition for growing space, and it is no wonder the world is not overrun by ferns.

During the millions of years ferns have lived on earth, they have evolved other ways of reproducing. Because these other ways do not involve the sexual stage, where spores give rise to prothallia, and prothallia produce gametes that unite, they are called asexual (without sex) or vegetative methods of reproduction.

A small group of ferns that live in dry climates can reproduce without water. They produce prothallia, as usual. But the prothallia don't produce eggs and sperm, or if they do, the eggs and sperm don't unite. Instead, the prothallia produce buds, and the buds grow directly into new fern plants. Reproduction doesn't depend on a drop of water gathering under a prothallium. The fern has bypassed the sexual stage.

If a small, young Boston fern is planted in a large pot and given good care, it will fill the pot rather quickly. But it won't fill the pot by growing bigger and bigger. Instead, it will produce a great many underground rootlike stems that grow away from the "mother plant." These rootlike stems are called rhizomes.

As the rhizomes grow, they send up new ferns. Each new fern, in turn, produces more rhizomes, which send up more ferns. Before the original plant reaches its full growth, the pot is full of new ferns.

Here the fern was removed from the pot to show the rhizomes.

Rhizomes growing through the drainage holes produced new Boston ferns. Once such a fern gets established outside—from a spore carried by the wind, for instance—it can crowd out other plants and take over an area. In this case asexual reproduction supplements reproduction by spores.

The Boston fern's rhizomes grow underground. Another house-type fern, the Rabbit's-foot fern, has hairy rhizomes that grow above ground (and look like rabbits' feet). The rhizomes produce roots as well as fronds. If a piece of rhizome is broken off, it will take root and produce a bud from which a new fern will grow. Plant nurseries take advantage of this. When they want new ferns they cut a rhizome into pieces and plant each piece in its own pot. Soon the pots are filled with new Rabbit's-foot ferns.

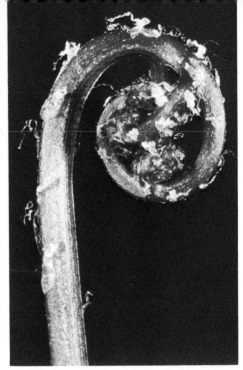

43

The word bulb brings to mind tulip bulbs and daffodil bulbs, but some ferns produce bulbs too. Tulip and daffodil bulbs develop underground. Bulbs on ferns develop above ground—right on the fronds. They are called bulbils.

One house-type fern that produces bulbils is *Tectaria gemmifera*, or Halberd fern. The bulbils form on both sides of most of the fronds on the plant. In due time they fall off, take root, and develop into new ferns.

44

Once in a while, the bulbils develop quite large fronds of their own before dropping.

The bulbils on *Asplenium daucifolium*, a house-type fern known only by its Latin name, almost always produce well-developed plants before they drop.

Some ferns have another way of reproducing—by "walking." A house-type fern called *Adiantum caudatum* does this.

When one of its long, graceful fronds reaches a length somewhere between eight and twelve inches, a bud forms at its tip. If the tip comes in contact with moist soil, it will produce roots and the bud will start to grow into a new plant.

Since the new plant gets some of its food from its mother plant, it grows rapidly. Soon there are buds at the tips of its fronds. Each new plant "walks" away from its mother, but stays attached to it for some time.

Plant nurseries raise ferns asexually whenever possible to save time and money. Nature seems to be leaning that way too. For a long time it was thought that the gametophyte phase, the sexual phase with the eggs and sperm, was an indispensable link in a fern's life cycle. But botanists now believe that in nature as many new ferns develop asexually as sexually.

Ferns are grown and loved by gardeners all over the world. Almost every country has one or more fern societies. Many of these publish various papers, bulletins, and books on ferns. Many also run "spore exchanges"—making spores of local species, as well as spores of house-type ferns, available to members in other parts of the country or the world.

Some of the better-known fern societies in this country are:

The Los Angeles International Fern Society
The International Tropical Fern Society
The American Fern Society
The South Florida Fern Society
The Delaware Valley Fern Society.

Their mailing addresses change from time to time, so if you would like to write to any of them it would be best to look up the latest address at your local library. When writing, don't forget to include a stamped, self-addressed return envelope if you want an answer.

If ferns fascinate you and you plan on raising a few, you qualify to hang a sign on the door of your room that reads, "A Neophyte Pteridologist Lives Here." That means you are a newcomer to the study of ferns.

INDEX